The Civil War

EARLY BATTLES OF THE CIVIL WAR

Linda R. Wade

ABDO
Daughters Publishing

Visit us at
www.abdopub.com

Printed in the United States.

Graphic Design: John Hamilton
Contributing Editors: John Hamilton; Alan Gergen; Elizabeth Clouter-Gergen
Cover photo: John Hamilton; Digital Stock
Interior photos: Digital Stock
Illustrations: John Hamilton, pages 11, 19, 22, 24

Sources: *Antietam.* Alexander, VA: Time Life Books, 1996; Bailey, Ronald H.
The Bloodiest Day: The Battle of Antietam. Alexander, VA: Time Life Books,
1984; Barnes, Eric Wollencott. *The War Between the States.* New York:
McGraw-Hill Book Co., 1959; Jordan, Robert P. *The Civil War.* Washington,
D.C.: National Geographic Society, 1969; Morris, Richard B., ed. Encyclopedia
of America, 6th Ed. New York: Harper & Row, 1982; Ray, Delia. *Behind the
Blue and the Gray.* New York: Lodestar Books, 1991; Reger, James P. *Life in the
North During the Civil War.* San Diego, CA: Lucent Books, 1997; Reger, James
P. *Life in the South During the Civil War.* San Diego, CA: Lucent Books, 1997;
Sandler, Martin W. *Civil War.* New York: Harper Collins, 1996; Smith, Carter,
Ed. *The First Battles, A Sourcebook on the Civil War.* Brookfield, Conn., 1993;
Shiloh. Alexander, VA: Time-Life Books, 1996; The World Book, Vol. 4, 1990.

Library of Congress Cataloging–in–Publication Data

Wade, Linda R.
    Early battles of the Civil War / Linda Wade
        p. cm. — (The Civil War)
    Includes index.
    Summary: Discusses the number of troops and casualties in each battle as well
    as the length and outcome of the individual campaigns.
    ISBN 1-56239-825-3
    1. United States—History—Civil War, 1861-1865—Campaigns—Juvenile
literature. [1. United States—History—Civil War, 1861-1865—Campaigns.]
I. Title. II. Series: Wade, Linda R., Civil War.
E470.W26 1998
973.7' 3—dc21   97-37486
                                                         CIP
                                                         AC

CONTENTS

INTRODUCTION

The United States were no longer united. The nation was divided. The Northern states were called the Union. The Southern states were called the Confederate States of America.

President Abraham Lincoln had to find a way to bring the nation back together. In his inauguration speech he called for peace and understanding between the North and the South. He said, "We are not enemies, but friends. We must not be enemies."

But the abolitionists of the North said that Lincoln did not go far enough. Southern leaders declared that the election of Lincoln was the worse thing to happen. They called for the states to secede.

Then secession came. South Carolina was first to leave the Union. Mississippi, Florida, Alabama, Georgia, and Louisiana soon followed. Jefferson Davis became the president of the Confederate States of America. War was the topic of many conversations.

Then both the North and the South decided they should control a little garrison in Charleston Harbor. It was Fort Sumter.

The stage was set for the first battle of the Civil War.

Left: Wagons filled with ammunition (caissons) line a wharf in City Point, Virginia, ready to be used by Union forces. *Facing page:* President Abraham Lincoln.

CHAPTER 1

FORT SUMTER

B oom!

It did not take long for those watching on shore to know what had happened. The Southern commander had issued an order. Northern soldiers must leave Fort Sumter. The fort was located on an island in the middle of Charleston Harbor. It was near the South Carolina shore.

Major Robert Anderson and 68 soldiers were inside the fort. They had been stationed there in hopes that their presence would delay any ideas of war.

The people of South Carolina were angry. They viewed the presence of Northern troops as aggression toward the South. So they cut off the troops' supply of fresh vegetables and meat. Before long, Anderson's men were down to crackers and water. Finally, word came from President Lincoln that food was being sent. He also sent a note to the South Carolina governor that no guns or ammunition would be delivered.

That did not satisfy the leaders of the Confederacy. They wanted all the Union soldiers out of their harbor. So Confederate President Jefferson Davis ordered Southern forces to capture Fort Sumter. General Pierre Beauregard was the Southern officer in charge. He demanded that Major Anderson remove his flag and men from the harbor. He had one hour! Major Anderson refused to surrender.

At 4:30 a.m. on April 12, 1861, a cannon rang out. Fort Sumter had been only a dark shape in the Charleston Harbor. Now it was lit up by exploding shells. Fires burned bright.

After 34 hours, a white flag appeared over the fort. Walls of the fort were shattered by cannon balls. The Union cannons were not powerful enough to reach the Confederates.

The Montgomery *Daily Advertiser* said that the battle was a "thrill of joy to every man in the South." Confederate soldiers were happy.

The North was stunned. They were eager to fight back.

The only casualty of the battle was a Confederate horse. It would be said later that "Fort Sumter was a bloodless opening to the bloodiest war in United States history."

The Confederate flag flies over Fort Sumter the day after the rebel victory.

CHAPTER 2

THE FIRST BATTLE OF MANASSAS— BULL RUN

Many of the battles of the Civil War, or the War Between the States, as it is often called in the South, have two names. This first big battle is an example. Southern leaders usually chose the name of the nearest town (Manassas, Virginia). Northern leaders often chose the name of a nearby stream or creek (Bull Run).

The morning of July 21, 1861, dawned bright and clear. The day promised to be hot. Both armies were prepared to launch an attack. Each planned to assault the enemy's left flank. The Confederate commander was General Beauregard. General Irvin McDowell led the Union forces.

The Union plan of attack called for troops to cross Bull Run at two different places. Confederate soldiers watched the movement from a hill. A warning message was sent by a flag signal. This was called "wigwag." Upon receiving the message, the rebels met the Yankees. They fought on both sides of Bull Run. They struggled for control of an important bridge, simply called the "Stone Bridge."

Confederate General Thomas Jackson came with more troops. He saw what was happening and positioned his men to wait for the enemy. General Barnard Bee pointed to this brigade and shouted, "Look! There is Jackson standing like a stone wall! Rally behind the

Confederate General Thomas "Stonewall" Jackson got his nickname holding off a Union attack at the Battle of Manassas.

Virginians!" Though Bee soon fell mortally wounded, his words did not die. "Stonewall" Jackson and the "Stonewall Brigade" went into battle fully intending to defeat the Union forces.

During many of the Civil War battles, it was not unusual for town people to watch the fighting. They cheered for their side. The North was so sure of a victory at Bull Run that congressmen brought their ladies. Society leaders from Washington, D.C., came too. They wanted to see the South run.

Then came the surprise! The North turned and made a hasty retreat. In their frantic rush the fleeing troops mixed in with the spectators. The people were scared. They screamed and tried to get away. Horses reared up. The people expected to be stampeded and killed. They all ran because they thought the rebels were after them. However, when they turned and looked, they saw no Confederates. What they did see were dead and dying men out in the fields.

The Union suffered about 2,900 casualties: killed, wounded, captured, and missing soldiers. The Confederates suffered about 2,000. However, they captured many guns, rifles, and other supplies and equipment. These were the things the Northern troops dropped during their retreat.

This battle changed many things about the Civil War. The uniform color of the Union soldier was blue. The Confederates wore gray. Some of the soldiers were trained locally and wore uniforms of the wrong color. A regiment of Highlanders from New York City came in kilts. Some North African soldiers from the French army appeared in baggy trousers.

Even the flags in this battle were not helpful. From a distance, the official Confederate Stars and Bars with a blue field and three stripes looked too much like the Union flag. In the heat of battle, Union troops shot Northern soldiers. Confederates fired into Southern ranks.

After this battle the Confederates adopted a new battle flag. It is the one we see today. Also, both sides chose uniforms of a distinctive color. The Union wore blue and the Confederates wore gray.

There was no longer any doubt that Virginia would secede. A mob marched on the State House in Richmond. They tore down the Stars and Stripes and put up the Stars and Bars.

Artillery, gunners, and infantry cross a river on a pontoon boat.

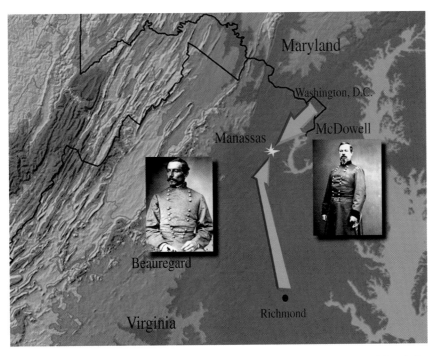

The first Battle of Bull Run, near Manassas Junction, Virginia.

On April 15, Lincoln put out a call for 75,000 volunteers. Posters called for sharpshooters. They were promised kisses from the girls and suits of clothes. Whole towns often signed up. There were big parades. They drilled night and day for at least two weeks. Then they marched off to war with feelings of both joy and sorrow. They did not know when they would return.

In Galena, Illinois, Ulysses S. Grant signed up at $4.20 per day. He was to play a very important role in the Civil War.

Tennessee, Arkansas, and North Carolina now joined the Confederacy. So many Southerners volunteered for the war that one-third were sent home.

As soldiers marched through a town, the bugles sounded. Citizens and ladies came out and waved their handkerchiefs for Jefferson Davis and the Confederacy. "It's worth soldiering for all this," they said.

Confederate General Robert E. Lee of Virginia, commander of the Southern forces.

On April 18, President Lincoln called Robert E. Lee of Virginia the most promising officer in the regular army. Lincoln offered him field command of the entire Union army. Before Lee could reply, however, Virginia seceded. At midnight, Lee wrote a letter of resignation to the president.

Soon, Lee was called by the governor of Virginia and asked to take command of the Southern forces. Lee accepted. When he had to choose, he could not fight against his home state (or country, as he called it).

CHAPTER 3

WAR'S BRUTAL REALITY

The staggering reality of war finally began to set in. Soldiers wrote letters home and talked about their dead friends. They now expressed fear of battle. Yet they were brave. Each side had a cause. In defeat, they were embarrassed. In victory, they were confident that in the end their cause would win.

After the Battle of Bull Run (Manassas), President Lincoln asked Major General George B. McClellan to train the Union troops. His men had successfully fought several small battles along the Ohio River. Northern morale improved. McClellan used these victories to recruit, train, and equip a 100,000-man force called the Army of the Potomac.

Union General George B. McClellan led the Army of the Potomac.

The devastating effect of a 32-pound artillery shell.

As the various units moved about, there were little battles when the two sides met. Each time the results were more casualties.

During the summer of 1861, the Confederacy realized that they badly needed Missouri. A rebel force of 11,000 advanced on Springfield. Men from Texas, Louisiana, Arkansas, and Missouri made up this unit. There were cowboys and coonskin-hatted mountain men bearing squirrel guns. In command of this group was Brigadier General Ben McCulloch of Texas. He was a colorful man in a snowy five-gallon hat, boots, and gray velvet coat with yellow cuffs and lapels.

At Springfield, about 5,400 Union men under General Nathaniel Lyon marched by night to surprise the rebels. The two sides clashed as the sun rose at Wilson's Creek. They were 10 miles southwest of the city. The battle lasted five hours. Casualties totaled 2,500. The Yankees were defeated again.

By the first anniversary of the war, many battles had been fought. Both sides had won. Both sides had lost. One big loss for the South came on January 19, 1862. It happened in the little town of Mill

Springs, Kentucky. In this battle, the rebel defeat meant a gap in the Confederate line of defense in the Tennessee-Kentucky area. This clash proved invaluable to the North. They captured 10 cannons, 100 wagons, and over 1,000 horses. They were also able to get many boats as well as guns and ammunition.

Tennessee saw many battles too. Fort Donelson was one of the biggest. It was on the Cumberland River. On February 12, General Grant's forces of 40,000 encircled the hills around Fort Donelson and the town of Dover, Tennessee. The federal gunboats moved into position to attack from the river.

For two days, additional troops and ships were added. The battle resulted in a victory for the North. There were many deaths. The Union now controlled the Cumberland and Tennessee Rivers. General Grant was promoted to Major General of Volunteers.

For the Confederacy, this was a major defeat. Many civilians attempted to flee the area.

On February 14, Lincoln's secretary of war issued orders releasing political prisoners. If released, the men had to take an oath of allegiance to the United States. They could no longer fight. On March 8, there was a battle at Pea Ridge, Arkansas. Two Confederate commanders were killed.

At the same time, out in Chesapeake Bay, naval warfare was about to change. The Confederate wooden steamer named the *Merrimac* had been converted into an ironclad. Officially, her new name was the *Virginia*. Now the ship had slanting iron walls that measured three inches thick rising from the deck. A cannon poked out of the four portholes on each side of the ship. She also had a bow gun and a stern gun. An arrow-shaped ram jutted from her bow like a huge iron beak. Her enormous weight put her low in the water. She appeared as a metal sea monster. One lieutenant wrote that she looked like a "half-submerged crocodile." Even though the ship had been renamed, it was still referred to as the *Merrimac*.

As the huge *Merrimac* entered Chesapeake Bay, she headed straight toward the wooden ships. They fired their guns, but the shots bounced off her thick sides. Finally, she turned and blasted the Union ship, *Congress*.

For the rest of the day, the iron monster fired at all the Northern ships in the bay. Because she was so big and hard to maneuver, the Union ships were often able to get away. Even the *Congress* had been able to get to shallow water, where the low-riding *Merrimac* could not follow.

However, the *Cumberland* received a crucial blow. After exchanging gunfire, the *Merrimac* rammed the wooden ship with her iron arrow-shaped bow. It remained stuck in the side of the *Cumberland*. Dead men covered the deck. Finally, the ship sank, carrying men to sea graves.

The Confederate ironclad *Merrimac* (left) trades cannon fire with the Union's iron-hulled *Monitor* (right).

Inside the *Merrimac*, men were extremely warm. Captain Buchanan went outside. He was struck by a rifle bullet and seriously wounded. A young lieutenant named Catesby Jones took command. Since it was getting dark, he ordered the *Merrimac* back to the Elizabeth River for the night.

The North had also been building an ironclad ship. It was called the *Monitor*. Not only did it have iron sides, it also had a motor-driven turret that contained guns. The moving turret permitted a captain to aim his guns at an enemy regardless of the position of his ship.

Back on the *Merrimac*, Lieutenant Jones had plans to wreck the remaining Northern ships. As he neared the *Minnesota*, a strange-looking new ship appeared. Confederate Lieutenant James Rochelle described the *Monitor* as "an immense shingle floating in the water, with a gigantic cheesebox rising from its center."

The captains of the two ships seemed to look each other over. The Southern *Merrimac* was much larger, about the length of a football field. It weighed more than twice as much as the *Monitor*.

And then the great battle between the *Monitor* and the *Merrimac* began. They moved around firing at each other. Most of the time they were less than 50 yards apart, yet neither could do any real damage. They even touched on several occasions. Inside the two vessels, the men suffered from the intense heat and noise.

Finally, both ships simply left the area. Neither ship was badly damaged. No one was killed. Both captains thought they had won. The day had been long, and was the first battle of ironclad ships.

While all the fighting was going on, President Lincoln was also dealing with a family illness and death. His son, Willie, had died on February 20. His wife was grief stricken. But Lincoln barely had time to grieve for the son he loved so much. He had to attend to his heavy presidential duties.

CHAPTER 4

SHILOH AND BEYOND

During the early months of 1862, Thomas "Stonewall" Jackson did an outstanding job with his men. Between March 23 and June 9, he marched 676 miles (1,088 km) and faced small skirmishes almost daily. He also fought five larger battles. He out-maneuvered men from three Union commands who were trying to catch him.

One of the big battles of the spring of 1862 was the Battle of Shiloh, or Pittsburgh Landing, in Tennessee. It happened on April 6 and 7. A surprise Confederate attack upon the army of General Grant at Shiloh on the Tennessee River caught the Union troops unprepared. A furious battle developed. One Union man wrote, "The soldiers came on and on." One rebel soldier said, "They mowed us down at every volley." Another called the place a "hornets' nest."

General Albert Sidney Johnston was hit, and bled to death. General Beauregard took command. He turned his 62 cannons into the hornets' nest and fired. Splintered trees and shattered men were all that remained when the smoke cleared.

Union General Ulysses S. Grant.

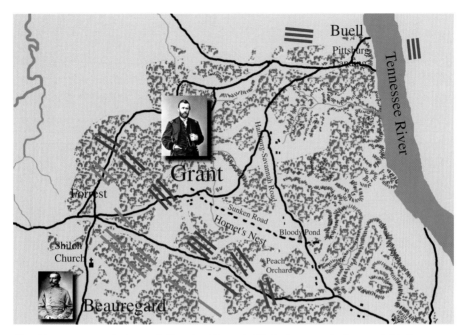

On the second day of the battle at Shiloh, a reinforced Union force under the command of General Ulysses S. Grant defeated Confederate troops led by General Pierre Beauregard.

That night, cries of the wounded reached those who had somehow survived. "Water," they moaned. Then it rained. By morning, Grant managed to rally his men. He called up reinforcements and turned the tide of the battle in favor of the North.

The two-day battle cost many lives. Losses totaled 13,047 for the North, 10,694 for the Confederates.

Dead and wounded men lay everywhere. General Grant said the ground was so covered with dead bodies that you could walk across the whole area without touching the ground.

While war raged all over the country, Congress was still working on the slave issue. On April 11, 1862, the House of Representatives passed an important bill. By a vote of 93-39, they called for the gradual abolition (elimination) of slavery in the District of Columbia (which included the cities of Washington and Georgetown). President Lincoln signed the bill five days later.

Frederick Douglass gave speeches across the country. He said the war was about nothing but slavery. President Lincoln still insisted the war being fought was about the Union.

In the West, a naval battle affected the Mississippi River. The battle began on April 24. The Confederate ship, *Louisiana,* blasted at *Hartford*, the ship of Union Flag Officer David G. Farragut. One federal officer described the predawn engagement as "the breaking up of the universe with the moon and all the stars bursting in our midst." However, Farragut's troops succeeded in capturing forts and winning the battle. On April 25, he steamed into the harbor of New Orleans. His victory put the Confederacy's greatest port and largest city in Union hands. It provided a southern river base for the Union. Now they had more control on the Mississippi River.

Fort Pulaski was on an island near the mouth of the Savannah River in Georgia. Confederates held the fort. But the federal troops surrounded it. The rebels had enough supplies to hold them for six months. However, the North was unwilling to conduct a long siege. They demanded that the South surrender. Colonel Charles Olmstead, the Confederate commander, sent his answer: "I am here to defend the fort, not to surrender."

Union Admiral David G. Farragut established control of the Mississippi River by capturing the Confederate harbor of New Orleans.

At 8:10 a.m., on April 19, the North opened fire. The bombardment lasted 30 hours. Cannon fire was so heavy that it peeled off Fort Pulaski's seven-feet (2 m) tall, six-inch (15 cm) thick masonry walls. Olmstead realized that the fort's powder magazines could now be hit. Everything would be blown away. Rather than risk a catastrophic explosion, Olmstead raised a white flag.

President Lincoln told Major General George B. McClellan to go on to Richmond, Virginia. This was the Confederate capital. McClellan said he was not ready. Confederate leaders began to call him "The Creeper."

Early in April, McClellan finally began to move. He had 121,000 men and 14,592 horses and mules. There were tons of provisions and 1,151 guns. It took 400 boats and three weeks to land it all. The men set in and prepared for battle. They were so close that they could hear the alarm bells ringing in the city. But no one knew just when the attack would come.

Two generals led the Southern army in a brilliant series of battles. They were Joseph E. Johnston and Robert E. Lee. Johnston sustained serious wounds. President Jefferson Davis then replaced him with General Lee. Lee immediately constructed eight miles of earthworks. These earthworks were hills of dirt used to provide protection from gunfire. Lee knew that if he waited until McClellan received fresh divisions and put his big guns in place, Richmond would be doomed. He had to attack. Stonewall Jackson and his 18,500 men would help. June 26 was chosen as the day for the advance.

For seven days Union and Confederate troops clashed. There was the Battle of Mechanicsville. Another day saw fighting at Beaver Dam Creek. The Battle of Gaines' Mill cost Lee thousands of lives. It was the bloodiest chapter of the Seven Days. Some of the fighting was "muzzle to muzzle, and the powder actually burned the faces of the opposing men," wrote a Union colonel. The Seven Days' battles turned back the most serious "on to Richmond" drive yet mounted.

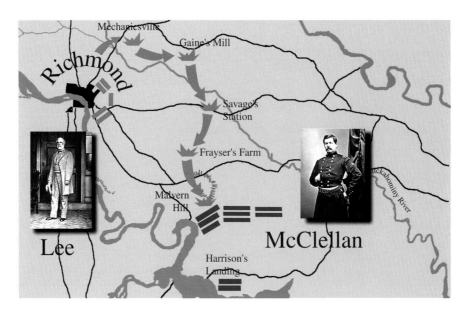

The Seven Days' battles were a bloody fight for Richmond, VA.

With all the fighting, Southern industry grew. Women made socks for Stonewall Jackson's army. Cannon balls had to be made. They used poppies to make opium for doctors to give injured men for pain. Needles were made from thorns. Spanish moss became rope.

Jefferson Davis put out a draft notice for all white able-bodied men from ages 18-35. However, if a person owned at least 20 slaves, he did not have to enlist. The men were not happy. They said it was a "rich man's war and a poor man's fight." Many cursed the Confederacy. Nearly one-half of those men eligible for the draft failed to show up. Meanwhile, in the North, former slaves were recruited for the Union army.

On August 29, the Confederate Army of Northern Virginia attacked General John Pope's Union Army of Virginia. It was the Second Battle of Bull Run. The Union attacks came in uncoordinated waves. Jackson pushed them back. This battle lasted two days. Once again, many men died. In the end, the South won another victory. The North retreated to Washington, D.C.

CHAPTER 5

THE BATTLE OF ANTIETAM

The North called it the Battle of Antietam (An-tee-tem). In the South, it was known as Sharpsburg. No matter what it was named, the results were the same. Thousands of men died. The battle came about for two reasons. The South wanted to gain recognition from Europe by winning a victory in Union territory. The second reason Lee marched north was to give relief to the Virginia farmers. It was nearing harvest time. He needed food for his men and horses.

A copy of Lee's orders was misplaced. Two Union soldiers found them. Shortly after noon on September 13, they were given to McClellan. Here was a golden opportunity for him to destroy the Southern army before it could come together again. McClellan should have marched that very night, but he waited until morning.

That night Lee learned that his orders were in the hands of the enemy. He was in a difficult position. He had only 19,000 men. Also, he did not know whether or not Harpers Ferry had been captured. He seemed to have one course of action open. He must retreat.

He headed for the Potomac River near Sharpsburg. Then a message came from Stonewall Jackson. Harpers Ferry had been captured. Jackson was en route to join him. Quickly the army turned, formed a line of battle behind Antietam Creek and faced their enemy.

But McClellan had not rushed at all. It took him two days to attack. Therefore, the Confederates from Harpers Ferry were able to reach Lee before the battle. In fact, several divisions joined Lee before the first gun was fired.

On September 17, 1862, General Lee knew he was greatly outnumbered by General McClellan's Army of the Potomac. And he was right. At dawn, the attack came. It was with brutal force. Wave after wave of Union soldiers poured in.

Perhaps the worst attack came from Major General D. H. Hill's troops at Sunken Road, which was near the middle of the Confederate position. The fight seemed more desperate there. It was called Bloody Lane. The attacking Union troops pushed forward in the face of terrific rifle and cannon fire. When they reached an

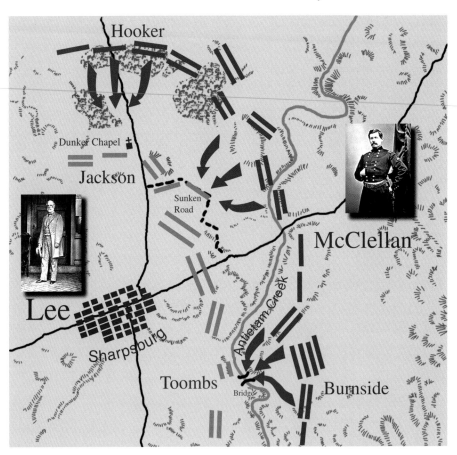

The Battle of Antietam was the bloodiest single day of the war.

The 96th Pennsylvania regiment marches in formation.

observation tower, they were able to shoot down the whole length of the Confederate line at Sunken Road.

Men were elbow to elbow, fighting one another. They were walking over their fellow soldiers to attack another. Many horses were killed. Sometimes the enemy would shoot the horse in order to get to the rider.

However threatened, General Lee's troops held their ground for some time. By dark, though, it was basically over. More men were killed and wounded than on any other one day of the entire Civil War. Confederate losses were about 10,000, one fourth of those engaged. Union losses were over 12,000, also about one fourth. That day went down in history as "the bloodiest single day of the war."

Had General McClellan attacked the Confederate lines on the 18th, the war probably would have ended. He had about 24,000 fresh troops. But the attack was never ordered.

In the Confederate camp all the leaders urged Lee to retreat. He decided to stay. He knew McClellan. He was determined that the Army of Northern Virginia was not to believe that it had ever been driven from any field. Not until the night of September 18 did the Confederates leave.

A victory of sorts did come at Antietam. President Abraham Lincoln issued a preliminary Emancipation Proclamation in September. It stated that as of January 1, 1863, slaves in those areas still in rebellion would be free. Lincoln could not actually do anything to free the slaves that he proclaimed to be free. Still, he had taken a stand, changed the nature of the war, and made clear that a Northern victory would mean not only the preservation of the Union, but freedom for blacks. Lincoln's action resulted in increased support for the Union cause.

President Lincoln meets with General McClellan and his officers on the battlefield of Antietam.

CHAPTER 6

WINTER AND FREDERICKSBURG

Geneval McClellan had hesitated many times when he should have pushed his troops forward. President Lincoln finally decided that he must replace McClellan as commanding general of the Army of the Potomac. On November 7, Lincoln chose Major General Ambrose E. Burnside.

The little town of Fredericksburg, Virginia, was halfway between Washington, D.C., and Richmond, Virginia. A railroad connected the Potomac River with Richmond. West of the town was a 70-square-mile (181-square-km) region of scrub oak and pine. It was known as the Wilderness of Spotsylvania. In order to capture the Confederate capital of Richmond, Burnside felt he must have Fredericksburg.

Burnside submitted a plan to attack Fredericksburg and then advance due south to Richmond. To do this, he had to cross the Rappahannock River. The bridges had been destroyed, so he ordered pontoons to be brought in. They came a week later. Lee was already there.

Burnside had already organized the Army of the Potomac into three large divisions. There were a total of about 120,000 men. The Confederate army of about 78,000 waited on the south side of the river, but not along the water's edge. Lee had also separated his men into different divisions. The left was the stronger part of the line. It rested on a steep elevation known as Marye's Heights. In front of the position was a wide canal and a drainage ditch, which the Union troops would have to cross. Behind the ditch, at the base of the hill, there was a sunken road. In front of the road stood an old stone wall just the right height to protect the defending troops while they shot over it.

In December, Burnside decided to go ahead with the bridge building. So under the cover of darkness, his men began putting six bridges in place. They got halfway across the icy Rappahannock. Suddenly, the town erupted into flame as a brigade of Mississippi and Florida troops opened fire on the bridge builders.

Unable to complete the bridges, Burnside turned his 150 cannons onto the city. When the smoke cleared, the Confederate army began firing again. Burnside now asked for volunteers to cross the river and drive the rebels out of town. Soldiers from Michigan, Massachusetts, and New York accepted the challenge. Hand-to-hand fighting began. Finally, after dark, the Yankees secured the city.

The following day, Burnside came up with new plans. One large division crossed the 400 yards (366 meters) of open ground and headed for Marye's Heights. The Confederates were concealed behind the stone wall. Later, one Southerner said, "A chicken could not live on that field when we opened on it."

Nightfall ended the killing. Confederate losses totaled 5,300 killed and wounded. Union losses were over twice as great. No attacker had reached the stone wall.

It was a very cold December 13th.

President Lincoln relieved Burnside of his command. But the war went on. When would it end? How long would men continue to slaughter each other? How long would cities be torn apart? How long could General Lee hold his army strong enough to defend the Confederate States of America? How long would it take for President Lincoln to unite the Union?

INTERNET SITES

Civil War Forum
AOL keyword: Civil War

This comprehensive site on America Online is a great place to start learning more about the Civil War. The forum is divided into four main groups. In the "Mason-Dixon Line Chat Room" you can interact with fellow Civil War buffs. The "Civil War Information Center" is especially good for historians and reenactors, and includes help with tracking down your Civil War ancestors. The "Civil War Archive" is full of downloadable text and graphic files, including old photos from the National Archives. When you're ready for more in-depth information, the "Civil War Internet" group provides many links to other sites.

The United States Civil War Center
http://www.cwc.lsu.edu/civlink.htm

This is a very extensive index of Civil War information available on the Internet, including archives and special collections, biographies, famous battlefields, books and films, maps, newspapers, and just about everything you would want to find on the Civil War. The site currently has over 1,800 web links.

These sites are subject to change. Go to your favorite search engine and type in "Civil War" for more sites.

PASS IT ON

Civil War buffs: educate readers around the country by passing on interesting information you've learned about the Civil War. Maybe your family visited a famous Civil War battle site, or you've taken part in a reenactment. Who's your favorite historical figure from the Civil War? We want to hear from you!

To get posted on the ABDO & Daughters website, E-mail us at "History@abdopub.com"

Visit the ABDO & Daughters website at "www.abdopub.com"

GLOSSARY

Abolition
To put an end to.

Army of the Potomac
Primary army of the Union.

Confederate Army
The Southern army.

Confederate States of America
Eleven states that withdrew from the United States in 1860-61. These states included: Alabama, Arkansas, Florida, Georgia, Louisiana, Mississippi, North Carolina, South Carolina, Tennessee, Texas, and Virginia.

Earthworks
Hills of dirt used to provide protection from gunfire.

Emancipation Proclamation
A proclamation by President Lincoln stating that as of January 1, 1863, all slaves in the territory still at war with the Union would be free.

Rebels
Confederate soldiers.

Retreat
The act of going back, usually used in defeat.

Richmond
Richmond, Virginia, the official capital of the Confederate States.

Secede
Withdraw from the United States.

Stars and Bars

Official Confederate flag.

Stars and Stripes

Official Union flag.

Union

Another name for the United States. Twenty four states remained loyal to the Union during the Civil War.

Union Army

The Northern army.

Washington

Capital of the Union. Part of the District of Columbia, which at the time of the Civil War included the cities of Washington and Georgetown. In 1895, Georgetown was annexed (added, or absorbed), and Washington became more commonly known as Washington, D.C.

White Flag

Flag raised for surrender.

Wigwag

Warning message sent by a flag signal.

Yankees

Union soldiers.

Crew of the gunboat "Hunchback" on the James River.

INDEX

DATE DUE